THEREFORE, GOD MUST BE ARMENIAN!

Sixteen Talks on Armenian Issues
(2007–2012)

John M. Evans

Former U.S. Ambassador to Armenia

Gomidas Institute
London

Illustrations printed with permission from Craftology, Yerevan (Armenia)

ISBN 978-1-909382-25-1

For further details please contact:
Gomidas Institute
42 Blythe Rd.
London, W14 0HA
England
Email: *info@gomidas.org*

The following sixteen talks and addresses were delivered by John M. Evans on issues related to the Armenian Genocide. Mr. Evans was the US Ambassador to Armenia between 2004-2006. This publication complements his memoir, *Truth Held Hostage: America and the Armenian Genocide - What Then? What Now?*.

CONTENTS

University of Southern California Institute of Armenian Studies

March 4, 2007

Thank you to Dean Peter Starr, to Provost Max Nikias, to the Honorary Chairs of this evening, and especially to Harout Sassounian for that generous introduction.

I find it unusual that anyone, even a government official, should be honored just for telling the truth. No one owes me thanks for telling the truth. But thank you anyway!

When I called the Events of 1915 by their correct name – which is "genocide" – I used a word the U.S. Government does not use. But as you have just seen in this short film clip, I knew what I was doing and knew it would have consequences. The decision was mine. No one asked me to do it. I stand by it. I have taken responsibility for it. As a consequence, I am free to be with you this evening!

None of us in this room is so naïve as to think that the official policy of states – even of the United States – is ever based solely on "the truth." As educated people, we also know that the truth can, at times, prove elusive. But when policy diverges wildly from what is self-evident, it ceases to command respect.

You may remember the Iraqi Minister of Information, who, when Coalition Forces were closing in on Baghdad, asked television viewers, "whom do you believe, your eyes or my words?"

Of course, when it has to do with events that occurred ninety years ago, we must rely on eyewitnesses like Amb. Henry Morgenthau, Consul Leslie Davis, and on historians – like Richard Hovannisian – diplomatic archives – and the survivors.

Ladies and Gentlemen, at the entrance to the State Department Library there is a quotation from Thomas Jefferson:

"We are not afraid to follow Truth wherever it may lead, nor [are we afraid] to tolerate any error, so long as Reason is free to combat it."

Unfortunately Reason – which tells us that there *was* a genocide in 1915 – is *not* free today to combat the false assertion that the deaths of 1.5 million Armenians came about as a result of mere "relocations," "excesses," "mishaps," disease and famine.

Turkey's official policy of denying the Armenian Genocide interferes with the process of seeking the truth; the U.S. policy of going along with this denial does not serve the truth.

I also believe in freedom of speech and of intellectual inquiry, as did the late Hrant Dink.

Many people have asked me why I decided to speak out about the Genocide. I am writing a book to answer those questions. I hope the story of my own intellectual journey may help others, particularly those whose names, like mine, do not end in "-ian", to reach a similar understanding.

In my book, I plan also to look at some of the things that could and should be done to deal with the great psychic and material wound of the Genocide. This is a difficult subject on which honest people can disagree, but I have several ideas already that I hope to develop. I will share just one of them with you this evening. For the others, you will have to wait for my book.

A Museum of Armenian History and Culture, including a Genocide Memorial, should take its rightful place among the other museums and memorials in Washington, D.C. It would be wonderful if this could happen in time for the centennial of the Genocide in 2015. Fortunately, some far-sighted leaders of the Armenian-American community have already acquired a site, centered on the oldest bank building in Washington, just two blocks from the White House. Such a museum could serve to educate visitors to the Nation's Capital about Armenian history and culture, and be a platform for social, cultural and intellectual life. The burden of financing such a museum should not fall only on the Armenian-American community. Congress should fund it in part, and others should be encouraged to contribute to it.

The Armenian Genocide will be recognized one day, not only by the United States, but by Turkey. In the meantime, there are many things that need to be done. First and foremost, the Republic of Armenia needs to be supported and nurtured, both materially and spiritually. The U.S. Government's official assistance programs, now also including the Millennium Challenge Account, have made a measurable difference.

Many of you personally and through your work have also made generous contributions and investments in Armenia. The new California office of trade promotion is now open for business in Yerevan, and investment is taking place. Thank you for all you have done and no doubt will continue to do for Armenia and with Armenia.

Obviously, not all Armenians live in the Republic of Armenia, and it is just as important that the needs of diasporans, especially young people, be met. For that reason, I want especially to salute the USC Institute of Armenian Studies. The Institute is doing a marvelous job of ensuring that Armenian history, arts and letters receive the serious academic attention they deserve, and of providing a vibrant center for the community of Armenian scholars.

Ladies and Gentlemen, as an "odar," I can say that the Armenian-American community is at its best when it joins forces for a common cause, as it did in 1988 at the time of the earthquake. There will always be divisions and differences of opinion, just as there are in any family. But to the extent that unnecessary divisions can be overcome, the community will become stronger and more capable of achieving its major goals.

So thank you for inviting me to speak to you tonight, for honoring me with this award, and for including my wife Donna and daughter Jennifer in tonight's banquet. Let us commit to working together in the future as we did in the recent past. Shnorakalutiun!

Times Square Commemorative Rally

New York, April 23, 2007

Good Afternoon, Ladies and Gentlemen! *Barev dzes, Tikhnayk yev Paronayk!*

New York City today continues a century-long tradition of sympathy for Armenia and Armenians.

Theodore Roosevelt called the "Armenian massacre" the "greatest crime of the [World] War."

Herbert Hoover, F.D.R. and William Howard Taft all served as trustees of the Near East Relief organization, chartered by the Congress in 1919.

The Rockefeller Foundation was an early and major donor to Armenian Relief.

Prominent New Yorkers like Al Smith, J. Pierpont Morgan, Fiorella La Guardia, and Cleveland Dodge were likewise leaders in supporting Armenia and Armenians. Most notable of all was the U.S. ambassador to the Ottoman Empire, Henry Morgenthau.

And while the Yale-Harvard Game cannot be exclusively claimed for New York, the proceeds of The Game in 1916 were donated to Armenian Relief.

———

The NY *Times* ran 146 reports on the Armenian massacres in 1915 alone.

More recently, the *Times*, in whose Square we gather today, has chronicled the continuing story of unbridled nationalism and its pernicious results:

* In an editorial entitled, "Turkey, Armenia and Denial";

* In its coverage of the assassination of journalist Hrant Dink;

* In its recent editorial condemning Turkey for blocking an exhibit on the 13th anniversary of the Rwandan genocide on account of a mention of the deaths of a million Armenians;

* In its coverage of the ongoing genocide in Darfur; and

* In a report on the slaying of three missionaries in eastern Turkey, who were bound hand and foot, and their throats slit.

We salute the New York *Times* for its dedication to printing the news, all the news that's fit to print – and then some – over these many decades.

We salute New York City for its role as a beacon of enlightenment in the past, the present, and the future.

And we salute Armenian-Americans of the New York and Tri-State area for their contributions to the arts, the professions and the economy.

And on this Remembrance Day 2007, we bow our heads in memory of all victims of genocide, including the most recent, the late Hrant Dink.

Remarks at Bipartisan Commemorative Assembly on Capitol Hill

Washington, D.C., April 28, 2007

Congressmen Knollenberg and Pallone, distinguished Members of Congress, Leaders of the Armenian-American community, Ladies and Gentlemen:

An unforgettable figure at the start of the Iraq war was Information Minister Muhammad Said al-Sahhaf. Minister al-Sahhaf vehemently and repeatedly denied that the U.S. Army was taking Baghdad, even as viewers everywhere were watching it happen in real time on their TV screens.

Minister al-Sahhaf became a caricature of himself, some would say a pop anti-hero, when he famously asked, "Whom do you believe, your eyes or my words?"

In some circles, al-Sahhaf might be put forward as a role model: the ultimate loyalist sticking to the official line come hell or high water. He set a certain perverse Orwellian standard.

I confess: I failed to meet that standard when I violated the taboo on using the word "genocide" to characterize the 1915 destruction of the Armenians of Eastern Anatolia.

I made my statements in Watertown, at UCLA, in Fresno and at Berkeley, in February 2005, the same month in which Turkish novelist Orhan Pamuk declared, "millions of Armenians were killed in this country and no one but me dares to speak about it."

I would rather be lumped with Orhan Pamuk than with Muhammed Said Al-Sahhaf.

The Iraqi Minister asked, "whom do you believe, your eyes or my words?

When we look at history, we must do so through the eyes of historians, especially if we are talking about events dating back ninety years or more, instead of real time events.

And historians tell us, almost unanimously, that there was a genocide of the Armenians in the Ottoman Empire in 1915. Genocide scholars tell us the same thing, only unanimously. They did so most recently in their letter to the Congress of March 7, 2007.

For some years, it has been the policy of American officials to say that "no American official has ever denied the facts of what happened in 1915." That was a good start.

More recently, an unidentified State Department official was quoted as saying "we have never said it was not a genocide." That was even more encouraging.

And in testimony before the HIRC on March 15, Assistant Secretary of State Dan Fried used the term "ethnic cleansing." This was a major rhetorical shift that I believe has been inadequately remarked upon and insufficiently appreciated. Because...

Ladies and Gentlemen, ethnic cleansing is a crime against humanity. The Allied Governments called the Armenian massacres a crime against humanity on May 24, 1915.

Hasn't the time come for the United States to say what the Allies said then and what the eyes of historians tell us: that the forced deportations, murders and massacres of Armenian men, women and children in 1915 amounted to genocide?

George Will is credited with having said that, in the United States, when we say, "it's history," we mean that it no longer matters: like saying, "it's toast."

We all know that foreign policy cannot be based exclusively on history, or on "truth." That would be naïve. The foreign policy of a great state must be based on the national interest, a complicated calculus on which honest men and women can, and do, disagree.

But a foreign policy that does not factor in history is vulnerable. A country that does not know – or refuses to learn – the lessons of history is doubly vulnerable, because the past has a long reach, and lessons not learned can lead to future mistakes and miscalculations.

To paraphrase Senator John Kerry, in what I think was the true sense of the remark that was misinterpreted last fall, if we do not learn the lessons of history, we as a nation will get bogged down in places like Iraq.

And to quote Senator Biden, "A relationship that rests on a requirement of a denial of an historical event...[that] is not a sound basis for a relationship."

If we dare not call the 1915 events a genocide, we make it even more likely that current genocides – such as Darfur – will continue, and future genocides will occur. One does not need to quote Hitler's famous remark to make that point.

This is why the time has come, after ninety-two years, to call a spade a spade.

House Resolution 106 on the Affirmation of the United States Record on the Armenian Genocide should be adopted by this Congress.

Because History matters. Truth matters. Justice matters. And the United States of America is still, despite many setbacks and shortcomings, a beacon for human rights, justice and human dignity around the world.

On Receiving the Morgenthau Award of the Armenian Assembly

May 3, 2007

Mr. Morgenthau, Chairman Hovnanian, Professor Power, Ladies and Gentlemen:

It is an enormous honor for me to receive the Morgenthau Award this evening.

Like the Darwins in Britain, the Morgenthaus in America have been eminent for over a century. It is a great honor to have Mr. Henry Morgenthau III here with us tonight.

Mr. Morgenthau's grandfather, Ambassador Henry Morgenthau, was a giant of American diplomacy, of American history. He is a personal hero of mine, and of many of ours.

I have no illusions. What I have done to receive this honor is nothing as compared to what Ambassador Morgenthau did in his time to help the victims of genocide – although he called it "race murder" – and to chronicle the events he witnessed.

Had I not read Amb. Morgenthau's account – his story – I would not have grasped the reality of what happened in 1915. Had I not read Samantha Power's book, *A Problem from Hell*, I would not have understood the reality of America's response to genocide.

I don't often quote Maureen Dowd, but recently she wrote, apropos of George Tenet's book, "If you have something deadly important to say, say it when it matters, or just shut up and slink off." I thought the 90th anniversary of the Genocide was such an occasion.

Ambassador Morgenthau represented our country in another age, an age in which the United States was just beginning to mount the world stage as a major player. Today we are *the* major player. But that stage on which Morgenthau acted, with different props, has become the central one.

Think about it: how many of the problems we are dealing with today – I have in mind Mesopotamia, Cyprus, parts of the Balkans,

Israel/Palestine, much of the Middle East – are left over from the collapse of the Ottoman Empire? Don't get me wrong: I'm not calling for its resurrection.

Many of those problems show up clearly on the map: the division of Cyprus, the artificiality of post-Ottoman borders in the Middle East. And the European Great Powers had their role in all that, as they carved up the Ottoman Empire.

But one of the leftover problems is almost untraceable on today's maps, unless one can detect that the land border between the Republic of Turkey and Armenia is closed.

And to the east of Armenia there is an unresolved conflict over Nagorno-Karabakh that is not at all "frozen," but still claims lives month after month. And there was Hrant Dink.

The problem that Amb. Morgenthau confronted has a long reach into the present.

Turks and Armenians badly need to come to terms with the legacy of their shared history.

This cannot happen without a candid discussion of that history without political taboos.

Turkey and Armenia need to find a way forward, away from hatred and violence, and toward a future of cooperation, commerce, more and better democracy, and human rights.

The legal analysis that was produced under the auspices of the much-maligned Turkish Armenian Reconciliation Council, backed by the Armenian Assembly of America, I think, points the way forward to a better place for Armenians and Turks. The missing ingredient in the TARC formula was "the truth," however unattainable that concept.

But interestingly enough, a truth did emerge, unexpectedly, from the legal analysis that was commissioned through the ICTJ. The study concluded that, although "no legal, financial or territorial claim arising out of the Events could successfully be made against any individual or state under the Convention,"... "the Events, viewed collectively, can [thus] be said to include all of the elements of the crime of genocide as defined in the Convention, and legal scholars as well as historians, politicians, journalists and other people would justified in continuing to so describe them."

53 Nobel Laureates recently based their appeal to Ankara and Yerevan to establish diplomatic relations, open the closed border, and cooperate in various civil society projects on the formula of the TARC analysis. Their appeal included a call on Ankara to recognize the Events of 1915 as genocide.

The philosophy that inspired the TARC Study will be at the center of my book.

I also want to say that, although I completely understand why Armenia rejected Turkish Prime Minister Erdoğan's proposal two years ago to set up a commission of historians to debate the question of the Genocide, the more recent restatement of that offer, by Foreign Minister Gül – to invite third-country historians to participate, could be a useful thing.

As in the case of France and Germany, and Germany and Poland, it would be helpful to succeeding generations to arrive at something approaching a mutually agreed narrative of shared history. So while we should not retreat from our judgment that what happened in 1915 was genocide, we may want to encourage more work, and common efforts by experts, to understand those events more fully in all their horror and their banality.

Because History does matter, Truth matters, Scholarship matters – and Justice matters.

Raoul Wallenberg Award for Diplomatic Courage

Remarks to the Biennial Conference of International Association of Genocide Scholars, Sarajevo, Bosnia, July 12, 2007

Dr. Charny, Dr. Stanton, Officers of the Association, Scholars, Ladies and Gentlemen:

Thank you for selecting me to receive the Raoul Wallenberg Award for Diplomatic Courage. I accept it with all humility.

What I did to merit this award was nothing as compared to the true heroism of Raoul Wallenberg in wartime Hungary, the quiet disobedience of Hiram Bingham IV in Vichy France, or the principled determination of Henry Morgenthau in Constantinople.

Those diplomats were real heroes; and they are heroes of mine.

All I did, in 2005, was to use the term "genocide" in describing the events of 1915 that resulted in the virtual destruction of the Armenians of Anatolia.

Why did my statement cause such a controversy 90 years after those events?

And the larger question: how to deal with a genocide now far in the past?

For the purposes of study, everything is in the past, to differing degrees. What happened yesterday, or ten minutes ago, is as definitely in the past, in a *qualitative* sense, as what happened fifty or one hundred years ago.

But for purposes of redress, for purposes of ensuring justice, events that are further in the past pose greater problems, even if, as is the case, there is no statute of limitations on crimes against humanity.

The 1948 Genocide Convention gave us a workable definition of the crime, but it did not solve the problem of how to go about making amends in past cases. It is not, in the view of experts, retroactive; rather, it binds the States Signatory for the future.

In the case of the Armenian Genocide, the perpetrators of the crimes of 1915-23 are now by definition all dead – although a few of the victims are still with us. There is no longer any individual perpetrator who might be brought to justice. The opportunity for doing so was lost when the original Ottoman courts-martial were abandoned and the Treaty of Sevres failed to be ratified and was replaced by the Treaty of Lausanne.

And so the conundrum remains: how to make amends for the survivors of the Armenian Genocide?

There is no easy answer to this question, but I will attempt to answer it in a book I am currently writing. So far I have come up with nine things that could and should be done.

Although nothing can fully compensate the Armenian people for the death and destruction they suffered in the last years of the Ottoman Empire, the most important thing is simply to recognize the truth of what occurred.

Armenian activists have for years pressed for recognition of the Genocide by parliaments and states, with some success.

At last count, 219 members of the U.S. House of Representatives, that is, just over half, have signaled support for a non-binding resolution that would call upon the President of the United States to take into account the U.S. record on the Armenian Genocide and to properly characterize it as such.

Some progress has also been registered in the courts and in private settlements with insurance companies, notably in the U.S. and France.

More needs to be done, but, ladies and gentlemen, that will be the subject of my book.

In the meantime, let me again thank you for this Award.

[After I used the word "genocide" to describe the events of 1915, a committee of American diplomats voted to give me the Christian Herter Award for Constructive Dissent. But that award was rescinded, on a technicality. I still expect to receive it in the long run, which will probably mean after my death. There is precedent: Hiram

Bingham IV received it posthumously in 2002. So I am still hoping to receive it, just not too soon.]

Let me also wish every success to the participants in this Conference as they return to their home institutions and work to make this world a better and safer place, a world in which genocide will no longer take place – *and will not have a place* – in human affairs.

International Law and the Armenian Genocide: Recognition, Responsibility and Restitution

Remarks to USC Institute of Armenian Studies Symposium, September 8, 2007

Let me say a few words about the international political context of efforts to obtain compensation for survivors of the Armenian Genocide and their descendants.

I will preface my remarks by saying that, while some measure of redress may be secured by pursuing class action claims against insurance companies or banks, as is already being done, to obtain compensation from the Republic of Turkey will prove much harder. On the other hand, there may be some other, non-judicial, remedies available, and I'd like to expand our discussion briefly to some of them.

As we all know, in the immediate aftermath of WWI, there was no international Nuremberg-style tribunal to punish the guilty and award damages to the survivors of the events of 1915-18. The Ottoman courts-martial that found the main perpetrators guilty and sentenced them to death *in absentia* were an important milestone, but did not complete the job. Most of those who carried out the Genocide were not brought to any sort of justice, and the land, property and wealth of Armenian families were not restituted. The Treaty of Sèvres, which foresaw an American mandate for Armenia, failed to win ratification, and that treaty is now for all intents and purposes defunct, superseded by the Treaty of Lausanne that says nothing about Armenia or Armenians. There is also a question as to whether the 1948 Genocide Convention can be applied retroactively.

My own view is that the Genocide Convention probably can *not* be successfully employed, *at least directly*, to obtain recompense from the Turkish Government. That was the finding of the analysis carried out under the auspices of the Turkish Armenian Reconciliation

Commission (TARC) by the International Center for Transitional Justice (ICTJ) in New York. I agree with many of you who consider that TARC was a flawed process in many respects, but I nonetheless believe that the ICTJ analysis, which concluded that the Events of 1915 did include "all of the elements of the crime of genocide," but that "no legal, financial or territorial claim arising out of the Events could successfully be made against any individual or state under the Convention," constituted a breakthrough. In particular, its finding that the element of "intent" was present on the part of at least some of the perpetrators was a very valuable point to have registered, and it bears at least *indirectly* on the overall political context.

The ICTJ analysis was very narrowly focused on the applicability of the 1948 Convention, and very carefully and clearly *did not rule out other vehicles* for seeking compensation, some of which we have been discussing here today. Any of the approaches chosen will take place in an international political context that may – or may not – be helpful, and that will itself be affected by the methods used and the goals pursued. In short, *how you proceed will affect how successful you will be.*

The international political context has, from the end of hostilities in WWI up to now, effectively prevented survivors of the Genocide from obtaining compensation from Turkey. Turkey has been and remains an important ally and partner of the United States and of all other major powers, including, notably, the most powerful state in the Middle East, Israel. And yet, as Samantha Power has said, Armenians have largely won the historical debate and the battle in the court of public opinion, just not with Washington and Ankara.[*] Increased public awareness of the facts of what happened in 1915 and growing sympathy for the Armenian argument has changed to some extent the context in which efforts to seek redress can now take place. If, as seems increasingly likely, the U.S. House of Representatives approves H. Res. 106, the political context will be marginally altered again. But then what? There still will remain the frustrating issue of

---

[*] Samantha Power, as quoted in the Boston *Globe*, "Armenian Campaign Aided by New Forces," by Keith O'Brien, August 26, 2007

compensation or redress. We should recall that the failure of the Lausanne Treaty to win ratification by the U.S. Senate did not stop the Coolidge Administration from entering into diplomatic relations with the young Turkish Republic.

If the goal sought is the return of territory – the six traditionally Armenian provinces of eastern Anatolia – resistance on the part of Turkey and of the international community will be fierce. States jealously protect their own territorial integrity and that of other states. Not only is the Sèvres Treaty now a dead letter, but multiple subsequent treaties have recognized and reinforced the Republic of Turkey's current boundaries. Of particular note in this context is the Washington Treaty that established NATO, in particular Articles IV concerning territorial integrity and V committing each ally to consider an attack on the territory of another to be an attack on itself. There is also the politically binding Helsinki Final Act of 1975 that commits the participating states to respect each other's territorial integrity. So the goal of recovering territory is probably not realizable, and to pursue it may actually harm the international political context. I tend to agree with what Taner Akçam has said, that the *territorial* question, as opposed to that of *responsibility for the Genocide*, should be considered closed. But if – and this is a big "if" – the two questions, that of Turkey's sovereignty and boundaries and that of responsibility for the Genocide, can be disentangled, progress can perhaps slowly be made.[*]

If the goal is to seek reparations from Turkey for survivors of the Genocide by means of a court settlement or arbitration, the resistance of the international community is likely to be slightly less fierce, but still, on the whole, hostile. The obstacles to getting the matter before a competent court are immense, as we have heard. The Republic of Armenia is unlikely to initiate a proceeding at the International Court of Justice in The Hague, and no other state is likely to take this step. The unilateral reservations that the United States insisted upon at the time of its ratification of the 1948 Genocide Convention

---

[*] Taner Akçam, as quoted in Harvard Crimson on-line, 3/15/2007.

would, very likely, be cited by the Government of Turkey as an excuse not to submit to the jurisdiction of the International Court. It is not widely understood that parties to proposed arbitration at The Hague must agree to it. Some of you may know that Turkish members of the TARC at one point called for submitting the dispute over the "Events of 1915" to the Court for arbitration. This idea did not win favor, and it might very well be a bad idea, as the Court is better suited to arbitrating technical issues than major historical ones. The efforts Turkey has apparently been making to prevent adoption of H. Res. 106 would pale by comparison to the full-court press that Ankara would make to avoid being hauled into any court likely to reach a judgment that would favor Armenia. And given the dense web of institutional, political and economic ties that bind Turkey to its allies and partners, the general international resistance to any such international court proceeding would be formidable.

That brings me back to the question of other, non-judicial options, all of which would involve talking to the Turks. It is my view that, if a suitable venue and mechanism could be found for conducting serious negotiations with Turkey, the international community – which would like to see the dispute resolved – would applaud, and international public opinion would change from being hostile to being supportive.

Alfred de Zayas has written of securing "a measure of compensation" for the survivors of the Genocide and their heirs. I can imagine fleshing out his phrase by designing a package of compensation that might include a mixture of steps to be taken and payments to be made, *as the result of a process of negotiation.* Just as 95% of all legal disputes in the United States are eventually resolved through out-of-court settlements, so this dispute stands to be resolved more effectively by negotiation than by means of court action, which, as we have seen, is very difficult to organize without a powerful international champion.

Given the intense pressure that Turkey has felt in recent months and years over its official denial of the Genocide, the authorities in

Ankara just might in future be motivated to settle this long-standing dispute, which is clearly a diplomatic and political problem for them.

I know that some will object in principle to talking to the Turks, saying that for the victim to have to negotiate with the perpetrator is not fair or appropriate. After all, the Genocide was murder on a massive scale, not a case of pick-pocketing – although it was that as well. This is true, but international life is still largely a Hobbesian world in which the various sovereign states protect their interests with great success against the still puny threat posed by the international courts and tribunals they have reluctantly established and severely constrained. Holocaust survivors successfully sued the German and Austrian governments, but their relative "success" came as the result of negotiations, not the litigation itself. Nearly every time a judge in a case ruled, it was *against* the claims of the victims. It was the public, political and diplomatic pressure in the background that secured some measure of success. Payments were made and property restituted with a combined valued of close to $7 billion.[*] It is, I have to say, going to be much harder in the Armenian case, for several reasons: 1) because so much time has passed; 2) because there are so few survivors left; and 3) because we are dealing with Turkey in this case, not with Germany or Austria. Even in the case of the Holocaust, the survivors received relatively small compensation, and their heirs, nothing, unless the survivor had already been approved for compensation and died during the course of negotiations.[†]

Public and political support for Armenian Genocide recognition has increased most notably this summer with the change of position by the Anti-Defamation League and the American Jewish Committee. This is undoubtedly helpful. But just as significant may be the fact that the continuing Armenian-Turkish dispute represents an intractable problem for the international community. It intrudes into deliberations of the OSCE Permanent Council in Vienna. It crops up regularly at NATO and other international organizations.

---

[*] According to attorney Martin Mendelsohn, in a private communication.

[†] John Becker, Property Restitution Advisor, Office of Holocaust Issues, Department of State.

The international community, on balance, has an interest in seeing this issue resolved. As public opinion has gradually, and now even more decisively, started to incline towards universal recognition of the Armenian Genocide and renewed sympathy for the Armenian cause, the time may be right to think about talking to the Turks, negotiating rather than litigating, although one does not rule out the other; in fact, litigation and other threats of legal or political action can serve as a useful backdrop and catalyst for negotiations.

But if one is to think about talking to the Turks, there are two or three big questions to consider. First, who would be the actual parties to the negotiations? Second, what would be the goals of the talks? And third, how could such talks be structured and carried out? Here are a few initial thoughts.

The parties to such talks clearly must include the Republic of Turkey and the Republic of Armenia, but also representatives of the worldwide Armenian Diaspora.

Goals for the Diaspora should include, at a minimum, 1) recognition by Turkey of the Armenian Genocide and a clear and meaningful apology for it; 2) restitution, insofar as it is possible today, of Church and community property; 3) a credible procedure for restitution of private property through Turkish courts, similar to the procedures used in Central European countries after the fall of Communism; 4) technically "voluntary" – that is, negotiated – payments to survivors and their descendants; and 5) some serious contribution to memorializing the Genocide, as by a major grant of "seed money" for the planned Armenian Genocide Museum and Memorial in Washington. Of course, the Republic of Armenia should obtain its own primary *desiderata*, starting with the opening of the closed border, full diplomatic relations, and the restoration of normal transport and energy ties. Since Yerevan's interests are not identical to those of Armenians living elsewhere, considerable thought needs to be devoted to figuring out how to do justice to both, whether in two separate sets of talks or talks structured in such a way as to deal with both "baskets" of issues. The question of who would represent Diasporan Armenians in such talks is obviously a tough one, but it is theoretically soluble.

Some Armenian friends of mine imagine that Turkey might give Mt. Ararat back to Armenia. That is very unlikely to happen, but one could perhaps seek the designation of Mt. Ararat – and perhaps also the ancient city of Ani – as an area specially dedicated to international peace and friendship. Inspiration could be drawn from the Waterton-Glacier International Peace Park that straddles the U.S.-Canadian border. Another idea might be somehow to link Turkey's eventual accession to the European Union to simultaneous accession for Armenia, although that would bring in a number of other issues and might actually complicate matters. The Nagorno-Karabakh issue will undoubtedly also be in play, either directly or indirectly, and needs also to be factored into one's calculations.

For such negotiations to bear fruit, they would have to be supported not only by Washington, but by the European Union and the Russian Federation, at a minimum. Some state or institution would need to offer to host such talks and serve as a disinterested third party. Simply by virtue of being negotiations rather than a judicial procedure, direct talks would have a better chance of getting started, would offer more varied options for settlement, and thus a better chance of eventually producing something everyone could live with. Turkey surely would like to resolve this problem, which has been costing it millions to deal with. Given the increasingly evident failure of its current strategy, Turkey might well be ready at this point to consider talking to Diasporan Armenians, and even compensating in some way the descendants of survivors of the Genocide rather than high-priced Washington lobbyists. At this point it might be more effective to seek a technically "voluntary" payment by Turkey than to press for anything smacking of "reparations," although recognition of the Genocide and a meaningful apology of some sort should not be negotiable.

It is too soon to say whether the recent elections in Turkey that brought the AKP to a strong majority in that country's Parliament, and Abdullah Gül to the Presidency, will have any immediate positive effect on Turkey's position regarding the Armenian Genocide. It would be wise to assume that these changes will not include a softening of the official position, but at the same time to think how one might work to encourage the opening to greater democracy that the election results do seem to represent. The Armenian Diaspora has an opportunity, I think, to make a difference in this new situation.

In short, as we consider the various options for seeking redress through legal mechanisms, which have not been terribly productive in the past, I believe we should also keep in mind the possibility of seeking alternative solutions. The international political context will, in my view, be more supportive of a *negotiated settlement*; in fact, the international community would probably applaud even the attempt. And having at least the tacit support of the international community – a positive international context – should make a significant difference in the outcome.

I am aware that, at this symposium, devoted as it is to international law and the Armenian Genocide, discussion of what are, essentially, diplomatic – or negotiated – approaches, may be unwelcome. Still, it seems to me that one must not lose sight of the reality that such approaches may in the end prove more productive.

Freedom Award

Thank you, Ken [Hachikian], for that kind introduction.

Ladies and Gentlemen, *bari yereko*. And thanks to all of you for your support during the last two and half years. My wife Donna and daughter Jennifer, who are here with me tonight, also felt that support. We appreciate it very much. Thank you all. It is an honor to be with you this evening.

No one owes me any thanks for what I said on the subject of the Armenian Genocide. For me it came down to a moral – an ethical – issue. No one asked me to look into the history of the Genocide, which I did in some detail, or to speak out about it. Doing so was entirely my own decision. It was not a State Department "trial balloon" or plot. It was definitely not a slip of the tongue. I knew at the time what the probable consequences would be, and do not regret my actions to this day.

We left Yerevan just one year ago this month. Now that I am again a private citizen, I am free to speak to you tonight and to accept, in all humility, your Freedom Award at this First Banquet of the ANCA Eastern Region.

Ladies and Gentlemen, in terms of astronomy, tonight is the autumnal equinox, one of two times in the year when day and night, light and dark, are in perfect balance. In keeping with the theme of tonight's dinner, *Building the Foundation for a Secure Future*, it's a good time to consider the balance of history as well – and the balance between past and future – all while staying firmly grounded in the present.

Is the glass half empty or half full?

Let me remind you: I am not an Armenian; I am an *odar*. But let me at least tell you how I see it.

Let's start with the Genocide, although we could obviously start many centuries earlier. In the first part of the twentieth century, more than half of the Armenian population of Anatolia was slaughtered in what the vast majority of historians and experts agree was the first major genocide of the twentieth century. The tragedy and heartbreak of the Genocide were only compounded when the First Republic was briefly established, but then absorbed into the Soviet Union. I think we could fairly say that the glass was not only emptied: it was shattered.

Armenians of all walks of life fled to countries other than their historic homeland, notably to the United States and France.

But already in the first half of the last century, Armenians established new lives, built churches, married and raised their families. It was not easy, and no one seemed to sympathize with what they had gone through. But in the second half of the twentieth century, awareness of the enormity of the crime that had been committed in 1915 slowly grew. In 1981 President Reagan referred to the Genocide in a public proclamation, something most Americans do not realize. The House of Representatives passed resolutions in 1975 and 1984 recognizing it. Dozens of scholarly books, memoirs and oral histories were published. The battle for recognition was essentially won, as Samantha Power has said, in the court of public opinion, if not in the ministries of foreign affairs of many countries, including our own.

The glass was slowly filling up.

Today, there are some 226 co-sponsors in the House of Representatives for House Resolution 106, and it is only a matter of time before it, or a version of it, is adopted.

And in August, the controversy that broke out in Watertown, Massachusetts set off a chain reaction that led to a change of position regarding the Armenian Genocide by the Anti-Defamation League, the American Jewish Committee and other Jewish community organizations. Significantly, it was young American Jews who led the charge. This was nothing less than historic. Today being Yom Kippur – the Day of Atonement – we send greetings to our Jewish friends and look forward to more cooperation in the future.

But the most important thing is that an independent Armenian state has reemerged on the world map. Although it may be small, it is a free-market, emerging democratic state where all political parties – including notably the ARF – are now free to compete for power, and do so with enthusiasm. It is not perfect. There is lots of work still to be done there. But yesterday the Republic of Armenia celebrated its sixteenth year of independence.

Next year will mark twenty years since the Armenian earthquake. As tragic as that disaster was, it raised the awareness of ordinary Americans about Armenia and became the catalyst for a major program of assistance largely engineered by the United States that continues to this day. Some of you who visited my office in Yerevan may have seen my Washington *Post* editions for December 8-10, 1988, whose successive headlines showed a progression as the *Post*'s editors gradually pinpointed Armenia on the map. And you know that total assistance by the United States to Armenia has cumulatively topped $1.6 billion. The Armenian National Committee can take a large share of the credit for this achievement, and for ensuring that Armenia has not been disadvantaged in current U.S. foreign policy before or after 9/11.

Today, by the way, the United Armenian Fund celebrated its 144th airlift to Armenia, bringing the total value of humanitarian aid assistance delivered since 1989 to a whopping $500 million. This is another milestone, and another thing for all Armenian-Americans to be proud of.

The Republic of Armenia not only exists, but is growing stronger in almost every dimension: economy, population and political maturity. Although still only a "teen-ager" among states, it is growing up to be strong and healthy. Demographic trends are gradually improving, with fewer young people leaving and more immigrants arriving, many of them from Iran and other parts of the Middle East. The decision to amend the Constitution to permit dual citizenship for Armenians living in the Diaspora was a good one, and will prove its worth over the years. In this connection, it seems to me that it is time to push again for a bilateral tax treaty, as ANCA did in 2004.

Let me say a few cautious words about recent developments in Turkey. I am not an expert on Turkey. I do not speak Turkish, but I try to follow events there as best I can.

The murder of Hrank Dink last January was nothing less than a tragedy for both Turks and Armenians, and for all who care about democracy and free speech. It showed that extreme nationalism still poses a lethal threat.

But the recent victory of the Justice and Development Party – the AKP – in parliamentary and presidential elections, while it does not signal an imminent shift in Turkish policy, at least suggests that things can change in Turkey. In the long run, Turkey is bound to evolve in the direction of more democracy. Some Turkish commentators are already saying that the policy of denying the Armenian Genocide has failed. A time will surely come, sooner or later, when Turkish society will come to recognize the Genocide and progress will be made in Turkey's relations with Armenia and Armenians.

Let me be clear. I am not holding my breath; nor should you. But what is needed here is *strategic patience and persistence*.

Back to the original question: *is this glass half full or half empty?* Probably you are expecting me to say the glass is half full. But I will not be so bold as to say that. Each of us certainly has his or her own view. Clearly the glass is neither empty nor full. My suggestion tonight is to focus not on the glass, but on the wine. And then let's work together to fill it up. *Tsehr kenatse!* And again, thank you for this award [the Freedom Award of ANCA's Eastern Region] and for your support.

"Fierce Urgency of Armenian Studies"

U.C. Berkeley, March 29, 2008

I'm delighted to be here with you tonight to support the Armenian Studies program at UC Berkeley. Special thanks to Adam Kablanian and Stephan Astourian...

The case for supporting Armenian Studies might seem self-evident, after all:

* The Garden of Eden was in Armenia; therefore
* Adam must have spoken Armenian,
* and since Adam spoke to God,
* God must also have spoken Armenian.

This was, of course, the argument Father Chamchian advanced in the 18th century to prove that the Armenians were the "real" chosen people.

In fact, let's just take that next step and say God probably is Armenian.

Well, I'm only an *odar*, and, try as I may, I cannot become an Armenian, even if my last name is sometimes pronounced "Evants." But I can put forward three good reasons why Armenian Studies deserve support.

First of all, *Armenians need to be able to study their heritage, not only in Sunday School or at home, but at the university level.* Armenian history and culture are worthy of study in their own right. Armenia has a fascinating history and a remarkable literature. Making Armenian Studies available is even more important because some have tried to suppress the narrative of Armenian history, even to deny the story of Armenia's terrible suffering in the first quarter of the 20th century. That narrative, that story, deserves to be told, loudly and clearly, and with scientific and historical accuracy. I am not saying that Armenian Studies should be subordinated to Genocide Studies. What I am saying is that the price paid by Armenians in the Genocide cannot be fully comprehended without a sense of what had gone before, what was lost, what was put at risk, and what the consequences were.

Second, *Armenian History should be of particular interest in America, precisely because the history of Armenia and Armenians is so very different.* We commonly study ancient Greece and Rome because they are the foundations for our Western heritage. We study European history and literature for the same reasons. But we sometimes forget that one of the reasons to study other periods and other cultures is to liberate our minds from the provincialism of time and place.

The history of Armenia and Armenians should provide a useful and liberating contrast: a people that has lived through much of its history without a state, a nation whose glue is language, culture and religion – a nation whose experience, on many continents, is so different, in short, from the American experience. Studying Armenia, Americans may come to appreciate that the glue holding the American nation together is a set of civic and economic principles, while we are totally diverse by other measures of race, religion and culture.

Third, now *that Armenians have a state of their own,* in a complicated and potentially unstable area of the world, on the fringe of what Zbigniew Brzezinski and others have called the Arc of Instability, *America needs experts on that part of the world who have serious backgrounds in the history and culture of Armenia and the Ottoman – and Persian – Empires.* This is where the "fierce urgency" comes in. If you look at the problems we are dealing with today, a large number of them are in what used to be the Ottoman Empire. Some are in the former Persian Empire, and some are in what was the Russian/Soviet Empire. So I would call for more study, as well, of those histories and cultures. One does not preclude the other, and, in fact, Armenians have lived, and are living, under all three of those empires or their successor states. Surely the Armenian perspective on – and understanding of – that part of the world is useful, perhaps even uniquely so.

To recap: Armenians need strong Armenian Studies; non-Armenian Americans can surely benefit from them; and America needs them urgently.

For all these reasons then, let's all work together to strengthen the Armenian Studies Program at UC Berkeley and elsewhere.

Remarks to the 19th Annual Meeting of the Armenian Bar Association

May 3, 2008

Secretary of State Dean Acheson once noted that "a high percentage of those whose conversation one finds stimulating and enjoyable...are lawyers." He was talking about the fact that lawyers' training and work make them *better informed and wiser* about the human condition – *more sophisticated*, in short – than ordinary folks. The group I myself have found most stimulating and enjoyable to talk to is Armenians. So you represent a rare combination of the two! Thank you for inviting me to be with you today! Please remember that I am neither a lawyer nor an Armenian.

What I'd like to do is, first, to say something about recent developments in the Republic of Armenia; and, second, to discuss the issue of Armenian Genocide recognition and the prospects for obtaining redress. Finally, I will relate these questions to each other.

The concept of *free and fair elections* was first codified internationally at the Copenhagen Conference on the Human Dimension of the Conference on Cooperation and Security in Europe in 1991, where I participated as deputy to Ambassador Max Kampelman. The term "free and fair" was designed to capture the idea that not only should the voting on election day be *free*, but that the period leading up to the voting ought to provide *fair* access to the media for all candidates. The Office for Democratic Institutions and Human Rights in Warsaw was established in order to help the new democracies in the East meet these criteria. ODIHR typically fields both long-term and short-term observer missions aimed at assessing success in approaching each of these two criteria.

As important as free and fair elections are in the new democracies, including Armenia, an equally important criterion – perhaps even more important – is establishing *the rule of law, not only on paper, but in practice*. And in this area Armenia has been making important strides. Some examples:

The U.S. Government, through USAID, has been working with Armenian judges and lawyers to develop and implement sensible, yet ambitious, reforms that promote an *independent and more reliable judiciary*. We have been helping to improve the organization and effectiveness of professional legal associations in Armenia as well as supporting legal education reform through cooperation with a number of universities, particularly in Yerevan, Gyumri and Gavar. In my time as Ambassador, we supported the Chamber of Advocates and its adoption of a new Code of Ethics. I saw recently in the news that the Chamber of Advocates, at its recent General Assembly, had decided to join the Council of Bars and Law Societies of Europe. At the meeting of this European group on May 12th, the Armenian Chamber of Advocates will receive observer status. The Chamber has also adopted a strategic five-year development plan, again with assistance from USAID and the American Bar Association. I know that the Armenian Bar Association has also done a lot to support fellow professionals in the Republic of Armenia, and I hope that this important work will continue. In the summer of 2006, there were some very good appointments to the bench, and some interesting court decisions that constituted progress toward consolidating the rule of law in Armenia, in particular, decisions that recognized the important role of precedent.

But looking at recent political events, we have to say that the violence that broke out in the wake of the February 19 elections constituted *two steps backwards* for democracy, and two steps backward for Armenia. It should be clear by now that if the law is seen by the people of any country as a tool in the hands of the ruling group, rather than as a system of justice that binds both the rulers and the ruled, there will be problems. In the same way, problems will inevitably arise when it seems obvious to the electorate that elections have been rigged.

Now to the question of the Armenian Genocide, and then I will come back to the present.

On the question of acknowledgement of the Genocide, much progress has been made in the "court of public opinion." One might even say, as Samantha Power has, that the case has been won, even though H. Res. 106 has not yet passed the lower house of the U.S. Congress. On the even more difficult question of how some form of compensation might eventually be obtained, there seem to be two primary schools of thought.

First is the controversial legal analysis that was conducted by an as-yet-unidentified legal authority under the auspices of the International Center for Transitional Justice here in New York. That analysis, as you may recall, argued that "at least some of the perpetrators of the Events [of 1915] knew that the consequence of their actions would be the destruction, in whole or in part, of the Armenians of eastern Anatolia, as such, and, therefore, possessed the requisite genocidal intent." The ICTJ study went on to conclude that "the Events, viewed collectively, can thus be said to include all of the elements of the crime of genocide as defined in the Convention, and legal scholars as well as historians , politicians, journalists and other people would be justified in continuing to so describe them." But most controversially, the ICTJ study also concluded that "…no legal, financial or territorial claim arising out of the Events could successfully be made against any individual or state under the Convention." Note that this was *a relatively narrow finding. It did not rule out approaches not based on the 1948 Genocide Convention.*

When I read this analysis in the fall of 2004, I thought it represented a major conceptual breakthrough. The ICTJ legal scholars had not been asked to render a judgment as to whether the Events of 1915 constituted genocide; they had been asked only to consider whether the 1948 Genocide Convention was applicable to those events, a much narrower task. The conclusion that 1915 constituted genocide was apparently a surprise, at least to the Turkish members of the Turkish Armenian Reconciliation Commission (TARC).

But in 2005, on the 90th anniversary of the Genocide, Alfred de Zayas, a Harvard-trained lawyer now based in Geneva, came to Yerevan and presented a paper at the conference there that April. He has recently updated his work and it will be published this summer in a special issue of the Armenian Review. *To summarize, de Zayas argues that Armenian claims did not originate with the Genocide Convention of 1948 and that the Convention merely confirmed pre-existing international law and thereby strengthened the pre-existing rights of the Armenians.* He dismisses the question of whether the Convention applies to the Armenian Genocide as a "red herring," an attempt to "distract attention from the legitimacy [and justiciability] of the Armenian claims." De Zayas recalls the relevant provisions of the Treaty of Sèvres and the Nuremberg Trials, both of which affirmed "the principle that the crimes of massacres and genocide were always punishable and were not first created by recent conventions or statutes." De Zayas then goes on to cite some more recent developments in the United Nations that are relevant. We will all want to read De Zayas's article when it appears this summer in the Armenian Review. It is already posted to his website, *www.alfreddezayas.com.*

I personally do not think that the findings of the ICTJ legal analysts and De Zayas's analysis are mutually exclusive. I think both are valuable to have on the table.

But *the larger question is what can realistically be achieved.* Mark Geragos and his colleagues have shown that a certain measure of compensation to the survivors of the Genocide and their descendants can be obtained from secondary parties such as insurance companies and banks through the courts. This is commendable. But it is worth remembering that *even the survivors of the Nazi Holocaust did not win their compensation through the courts, but rather as the result of world public opinion and the diplomatic support of the United States Government, which negotiated settlements with the relevant states, Germany and Austria in particular.* There seems at present to be no big power champion for the rights of Armenians in sight, so long as Turkey maintains its policy of denying that anything resembling a genocide ever took place; however, *the court of public opinion is in session* and this may eventually change.

It seems to me important to press the case *precisely* in the court of public opinion, to enlarge the constituency for support of Armenian

Genocide acknowledgement while keeping political pressure on Turkey to take some form of remedial action. Turkey should, as a first step, establish diplomatic relations with Yerevan without preconditions and open the closed border. This goal can be achieved. But *I am frankly skeptical of the possibilities of winning significant compensation from the Turkish State in any court, although the threat of litigation can provide useful leverage.* So far as I know, there is only one court to which Turkey can be taken without its consent, namely the European Court of Human Rights in Strasbourg. But there are other things that can be achieved politically and in the "court of public opinion," and that, it seems to me, is where efforts ought to be concentrated.

This brings me back to the present-day Republic of Armenia. Without gas or oil, or other important natural resources, *Armenia needs to become nothing less than the darling of the West, the leading free market democracy in the Caucasus.* This is a tall order, but not impossible. The recent setback to democracy will eventually be overcome, but in the meantime it offers Armenia's enemies an easy target for criticism, and dampens the ardor of those who might rise to defend her. The sooner Armenia can reach her full potential as a free market democracy, the more persuasive her advocates will become in the councils of Western governments. And Western governments and legislatures surely will develop more sympathy for the Republic of Armenia if there is more support among voters.

To sum up, Armenia has many of the necessary ingredients to make herself nothing less than the darling of the West, and, if Armenia is well-regarded, there will be more political support for all Armenian causes, including recognition of the Genocide and making some form of amends. In the court of public opinion, all sorts of evidence can be introduced that might not be admissible in a court of law. Armenians and their friends should take advantage of that, and view the overall challenge as broader than simply a legal one.

Edmund Burke once said that "law sharpens a man's mind by narrowing it." I disagree with that and count on the superior sophistication of Armenian law professionals to facilitate understanding of my arguments today.

I again salute you for all that you do both here and with regard to Armenia.

In Memory of Vartkess Balian

Remarks at luncheon, August 16, 2008

Your Eminence, Rita [Balian], members of the Balian Family, friends and colleagues:

I am here at the lectern almost as the last speaker. Many, many words have been said today, and yesterday. And I find it ironic, but somehow entirely fitting, that, whereas Vartkess was a man of few words, we have heard so many words of praise for him, and the same themes keep being sounded: "nobility," "integrity," "grace," "generosity," all of these concepts which Vartkess clearly embodied.

Now let me just say that I am speaking here on behalf of a couple, because Donna and I knew Rita and Vartkess as a couple. If Vartkess was a man of few words, I probably heard fewer of his words because Donna was normally sitting next to him. But he was a smart man, and he found a way we could talk. While Rita would take the ladies to look at the art collection, he and I would very often sit with a glass of wine in the main room there, and I cherish my memories of those conversations.

Also, in Yerevan, in the "modest house," as Mike Lemmon put it, that we were pleased to live in, we always got together. It was understood that when Rita and Vartkess came to town, we would see them. We would talk about those interests that we shared. And, of course, most important on our horizon was, indeed, the wonderful work that Rita and Vartkess did and are still doing on the Armenian-American Wellness Center.

In Julius Caesar, Shakespeare had Marc Antony say, "the good that men do is oft interred with their bones." That will not be the case with Vartkess. His legacy is living on in the many good works that he and Rita have undertaken and which are still continuing.

So I urge all of you to think seriously about their call to support the Wellness Center as a living legacy to Vartkess. It's a wonderful, wonderful concept. And I think in some way — and this is perhaps a bold thing to say; I don't know whether it was intended or not — but everything good that Vartkess did in some way countered the terrible things that happened at the beginning of the twentieth century: caring about maternal health, caring about infants, the health of the family, education – all of these good things to strengthen the Armenian people in their new state. All of these things deserve our support.

And one last thought: I don't imagine any of us here expected to find so much in common with each other. We all knew Vartkess from our own perspectives in different ways, some from many years ago, some more recently, and in different professional capacities. But here in these last two days, which, Rita, you so generously organized for us, it has been an experience that none of us will ever forget, and we should capitalize on this discovery of the common values – Vartkess's values – that we also share.

So, as we go forward from this place and this sad time together, let's also rededicate ourselves to those common values and think – as Vartkess always did – of deeds, not words.

Introducing Nicholas Kristof at Gala of the Children of Armenia Fund

October 28, 2008

Ladies and Gentlemen, it is a great honor to introduce writer and journalist Nicholas Kristof to you tonight.

As a long-time and careful reader of Mr. Kristof's columns, I had not known until fairly recently that he was an Armenian. I just knew he was damn good at his job.

Mr. Kristof's reporting on the human slave trade and on prostitution in Cambodia had struck a chord with me and my wife Donna, who works on the international problem of exploitation of children through the Internet. I had been especially moved by his accounts from Darfur.

That Mr. Kristof turns out to be Armenian is just further proof that he has been doing the Lord's work, since we all know that God is actually Armenian. (To remind you of the logic here: the Garden of Eden was in Armenia, so Adam must have been an Armenian, and since God spoke to Adam, God must have known Armenian, so God must be Armenian...)

But seriously, our world – after the Fall – is no Garden of Eden. And Nick Kristof has been an insightful portrayer of our fallen world, with its terrible problems and suffering, its hypocrisies, and – remarkably, still - its hopes.

Mr. Kristof's dynamic and gripping exploration of global issues has earned him two Pulitzer Prizes. His twice-weekly columns in the NYT have focused the world's attention on global poverty, health, climate and gender issues. In recent columns, Nick has helped readers understand the potential global consequences of our elections.

Nick is a true advocate of global change. As one who has traveled the world and knows its myriad problems at first hand, he is no detached observer. He has been engaged, in the classic French sense of the word, "engagé." His career stands as a lesson to the rest of us in how to give a voice to the voiceless and challenge the powerful to listen.

My favorite quotation from Nick: "One of the principles of journalism is, you don't lie. You never lie."

Tonight COAF, with profound admiration, gratitude and humility, honors Nicholas Kristof by presenting him the 2008 Save-A-Generation Humanitarian Award.

Rockefeller Archive Center
Near East Foundation Board Reception

September 10, 2009

Long before I was named US Ambassador to Armenia, I grew up in a town that the Rockefeller family, specifically John D. Rockefeller, Jr., preserved for future generations, Williamsburg, Virginia. The motto of Colonial Williamsburg is "That the Future May Learn from the Past." When I was a boy, Williamsburg had no Armenians, to my knowledge, but there was evidence, in the form of mulberry trees, of a prior Armenian presence. You see, the first Armenian recorded to have come to the New World, one "Martin ye Armenian," arrived in the Virginia colony in 1619 to cultivate mulberries to feed silkworms for the production of silk. Eventually, tobacco won out…

A short distance from the mulberries is a remarkable building that was preserved by the Rockefellers through their investment in the Williamsburg Restoration: the Public Records Office. It is the oldest archival building in America and the first fire-proof one. It sits right next to the restored Colonial Capitol, testimony to the Founding Fathers' understanding of the importance of records in a democracy.

But Virginia is also where one of the earliest recorded acts of destruction of an archive in North America took place, only a hundred miles or so west of Williamsburg. A British raiding party commanded by Col. Banastre Tarleton swept through Albemarle County VA, in 1781, well aware that this was Jefferson territory. In addition to destroying Jefferson's crops and barns, and stealing his horses and some slaves, Tarleton ordered the public records of Albemarle County burned.

A Virginia historian later wrote, "It is hard to conceive any conduct in an army more outrageous, more opposed to the true spirit of civilization, and withal more useless in a military point of view, than the destruction of public archives." (Rev Edgar Woods)

In the Twentieth Century, examples of document destruction are numerous: one thinks of Talaat Pasha's burning of papers at friend's house before he fled Istanbul, Ahmet Pasha's order to destroy the archives of the Special Organization, the wholesale Nazi looting and destruction of Jewish and other archives, the Soviet archival deceptions that unfortunately continue until today, and countless others around the world.

When archives in Kosovo were being destroyed in 1999, the Society of American Archivists issued the following statement:

"Archives hold the valuable records of the accomplishments of a nation, of a government's action and its people's lives. Destruction of the archives eliminates a vital link in a nation's connection to its past and destroys a people's ability to learn about themselves and to defend their rights and interests." When archives are destroyed, the statement continued, it represents "an irreplaceable tragedy for all mankind."

Unfortunately, attempts to alter the public record are not limited to other countries and other times. Some have taken place in our own day, the most memorable being the missing 18 minutes of tape on Rosemary Woods' recording device in the Oval Office.

Sandy Berger, the former National Security Advisor to President Clinton, and an acquaintance of mine, first denied and then admitted taking five documents from the National Archives in 2005. He hid some of them in his trousers and others in a nearby construction site. Sandy was disbarred, fined, and required to do 100 hours of public service cleaning up debris in a Northern Virginia parks.

Another acquaintance of mine, Professor Allen Weinstein, was Archivist of the United States in 2006 when the New York *Times* first reported that thousands of previously declassified documents were being reclassified, apparently at the request of the Air Force and the CIA. While there may indeed have been some errors in declassification that needed correcting, the very idea that documents were being withdrawn from public view was disturbing. Equally disturbing, to some, was the fact that Prof. Weinstein, who had no experience as an archivist, was named to the job after the summary dismissal of his predecessor (John Carlin), and without any consultation with the professional organizations of archivists. It looked very political at the time, although I am glad to say that Weinstein overcame the early suspicions and acquitted himself well in the end.

Earlier this summer, a public interest group sued the National Archives for failing to ensure that e-mail records of the previous White House were not being kept for posterity. The suit has since been withdrawn, but it demonstrated that these issues are very much alive in Washington.

What all these stories tell us is that the public record, housed in a variety of archives, some public, others private, is a treasure of our democracy and of human history. We are wise not to leave it only to governments to house this treasure, on account of the propensity, alas, of people in political life to attempt to change the facts of history, to apply "spin" after the fact. The fact that the Armenian Genocide, as a matter of policy, is not fully recognized as such by the U.S. Government is a matter of deep concern to me, given the archival record and consensus of independent historians that exists.

That the records of Near East Relief have found a safe and welcoming home here at the Rockefeller Archive Center is a great and good thing, all the more appropriate given the long and active involvement of the Rockefeller family in the history of America's aid to the Armenians during the Hamidian massacres and the Genocide. The Dodge family and other families of New York and elsewhere are also represented in this collection. In closing these remarks, I ask that you join me in applauding both the original philanthropy of the Rockefellers and the Dodges (and others), and today's philanthropy which has made this acquisition possible. Let us salute all those who are helping not to destroy, but to preserve these archival treasures and, in doing so, safeguarding the historical record of American involvement in Armenia and the Middle East.

Remarks at Panel on Elective Body to Represent All Armenians

USC, November 20, 2010

Since the Treaty of Westphalia in 1648, some would argue even earlier, the Western World has been organized into states. At first these were monarchies or other feudal constructs, sometimes combined into empires, but as time and social progress marched on, they evolved into constitutional monarchies or republics. By World War I, it was clear that the days of the large European empires were gone. The great empires broke down into states based on the principle of national sovereignty. So Austria-Hungary yielded up Czechoslovakia, Hungary and Yugoslavia, as well as its core states of Austria and Hungary, and so on. The Russian Empire continued well into the 20th century under new management, but eventually fell apart into fifteen smaller states based on titular nationalities, but with minorities in every one.

Through the process of great states breaking down into smaller units, and through the process of de-colonization, the number of recognized states in the modern word now stands at 192. More than half of these, 103 to be exact, have come into being, or been reconstituted in some way, since 1960. And yet there are still numerous national and linguistic groups who do not have any state of their own. The count varies depending on one's definitions, but ranges as high as 1500. The largest such group is the Kurds, who number about 25 million world-wide. Other well-known, but stateless groups include the Basques and the Chechens. Groups that have a state have a great advantage in the world as it is constituted: they have a legitimate voice in world affairs, a legitimate mechanism for providing for their defense, and an organization for perpetuating their language and culture through education and other means, such as the arts.

But let's turn to the Armenians. Worldwide, the scattered Armenian population is estimated at about ten million, of whom around three million live either in the Republic of Armenia or the unrecognized Republic of Nagorno-Karabakh, known to many in this audience as Artsakh. We all know how it happened that 1.5 million Armenians in the Ottoman Empire were the victims of genocide in 1915, and how those who managed to survive and escape then made their way to places of refuge like France, the United States and Argentina, to name only a few.

We should recall, however, that the scattered nature of Armenian settlement did not begin in 1915. Leaving aside such interesting but statistically irrelevant cases as my own favorite, Martin ye Armenian, who was present in the Virginia Colony in 1619, it is well known that there were Armenians in the Indian sub-continent, in Persia, in Russia, in Italy and even in the Far East long before the Genocide took place. But the Genocide did two things: 1) it expelled a sizeable group of Anatolian Armenians into the world to fend for themselves; and 2) it wronged that group almost fatally through death, starvation and dispossession. This intensified the sense that Armenians are people scattered to the four corners of the world, without a homeland of their own, and now bearing a grudge.

What we see today is a displaced minority that has a serious and justified grievance against its erstwhile imperial masters, but is dispersed among the nations – here one should say nation-states – of the world. The Armenian Diaspora has a uniquely painful situation. Unlike the Jews, who were expelled from Palestine in antiquity, the Armenians have memories, cruelly interrupted, by death and destruction, sickness and orphanhood, of a way of life and a whole civilization that they were forced to leave behind less than a century ago. If the Jews could return to Palestine, claiming Jerusalem as the capital of the State of Israel, after two thousand years, how much nearer in historical time is the Armenian departure from what is now Turkey, and how much more immediate is their claim to recompense for their loss?! For while the Jews can point to Scripture in justifying their return to Palestine, Armenians have heard the horrific tales told by their ancestors and relatives, and can point to President Woodrow Wilson's Arbitral Award.

Some have pointed out that, because of the prehistoric migrations of most of the world's peoples out of Africa, East Africa having been the portal through which most of us flowed, we are all "diasporans" of Africa. In a strict sense this may be accurate, but a true diaspora yearns for a return to the ancestral homeland, or at least follows with interest the events taking place there, be they as mundane as football matches. Here the Armenian Diaspora is cruelly disadvantaged, because the true "homeland" of most American Armenians is not really the Republic of Armenia; it is an Armenia that has been virtually obliterated in what is now the Republic of Turkey. So while there is an Armenian state now in existence, it does not have the same associations and affinities that the ex-Anatolian Armenians seek in what used to be their fatherland, in Ottoman times.

When, as US Ambassador to Yerevan, I discovered that the State Department's Background Notes on the Republic of Armenia made no mention of the Armenian Genocide, even in the euphemistic terms favored by the Department for political reasons, I thought it might be because "Russian Armenia" was not the scene of the Genocide. When I mentioned this to Prof. Richard Hovannisian, he argued that, just as Israel represents all Jews, the Republic of Armenia can be seen as representing all Armenians.

There is logic to this, and if the Republic of Armenia appeared to be a more competent and determined advocate for the interests of Armenians worldwide, we might not be having this discussion. For the Republic of Armenia is a "really existing" state, as Brezhnev might have said. It is a member of the United Nations and other international organizations like the OSCE and the Council of Europe. Many national groups do not even have this degree of representation.

We have mentioned the case of the Jews. The question of how a minority organizes itself within another (host) country is not a new one. In Britain, the Board of Deputies of British Jews is the main organization that represents its constituency. In the United States, the many Jewish civic groups are represented by the Presidents of Major Jewish Organizations. And Armenian-Americans have two major lobbying organizations, the Armenian National Committee of America and the Armenian Assembly, among others.

It seems to me that the impetus to explore the idea of a world-wide elective structure to represent the interests of non-RA Armenians ripened during the football diplomacy and subsequent controversy over the Protocols in 2008-2010. What that episode revealed was that the interests of the Republic of Armenia and of the worldwide Diaspora were not fully in alignment. President Sargsyan imagined he was within his rights as the leader of the Republic to cut whatever deal he thought would benefit his beleaguered nation, and its close relative, the unrecognized Nagorno-Karabakh Republic from which he hails. But the Armenian Government, despite having set up a special Ministry for Diasporan Affairs, did not consult in serious and timely fashion with its diaspora-based constituents, and Sargsyan was greeted by angry comments and catcalls when he toured Diaspora communities abroad after the content of the Protocols became public.

Armenian Diasporans can do anything they want to do, so long as it is not illegal, but I think they ought not to lose sight of the fact that having an Armenian state is a signal advantage to them, so long as that state carries out its proper duties as their representative. What the episode of the Protocols demonstrated above all else was that Yerevan, as a whole, was not adequate to the job. Whether it was not fundamentally capable, not aware of the expectations of its overseas constituents, or simply caught in a situation it was not prepared for, Yerevan dropped the football, so to speak.

So what is to be done? In a world in which states write the rules and dominate the international scene, it does not seem to me wise to embark on the construction of what will inevitably be seen as a "non-state actor" in the current parlance. Even if the various hurdles of language, culture, religion, political party that divide the world-wide Armenian community could be miraculously overcome and a World Assembly of Armenians elected – by electors whose "Armenianness" could be certified to the satisfaction of all –it would not have the status of any state that meets the definition of a state, however small.

Even Andorra or Liechtenstein would still stand ahead of such a structure in terms of international status and legal rights.

The election of a world-wide Armenian body is not necessary to provide for many of those things that Armenians are accustomed to receiving from their "host" governments: defense, health care, fixing pot-holes, etc. Those "governance" issues are not the issue; rather it is how to 1) influence the existing Armenian State; and 2) enable that state to carry out its plausible function as a representative not only of its 3.2 million citizens, but of overseas Armenians. That is the challenge.

It seems to me that this goal is best advanced by a combination of the very tools and processes that are now already in use: by influencing foreign aid budgets in "host" countries, by raising the awareness of Armenian issues in general, the Genocide in particular, and by investing materially, politically and in terms of human capital to the existing Armenian Republic. It is, after all, the only "Hayastan" now on the map. In future there may be two Armenian states, Hayastan and Artsakh. And why not? There are multiple Anglo-Saxon, Francophone and Turkic states. But until that day, the Armenian Diaspora would do best to place its bets with Hayastan.

Professional of the Year Award of the Armenian Professional Society

November 19, 2010

Thank you to everyone, and especially to Mr. Stephan Bagboudarian, your President.

Some of you may be familiar with the Islamic idea that the buyer of a product should be informed of its defects. This concept is often observed in the breach, but, in that spirit...

You have chosen me as your "professional of the year."

I am highly honored, but I will argue tonight that your reason for selecting me probably had little to do with professionalism as such.

We will get to that.

As you know, I cannot claim to be an Armenian. I am only an "odar," even though some people in Armenia pronounced my name "Evants" and believe I must be Armenian.

I saw that Elizabeth Dole was your honoree in 2001, so being Armenian is apparently not a requirement.

First, though, I want to talk about what you and I mean by professionalism.

In general, we think of "professional" as the opposite of "amateur"; the dictionary defines "professional" as "conforming to the technical or ethical standards of an occupation."

It can mean "learned" or "skilled."

Professions may have special codes of behavior, like the Hippocratic Oath.

In the American Foreign Service, approximately one third of all ambassadors are actually political appointees, chosen by the President because of their success as fund-raisers.

Career Foreign Service Officers refer to themselves as "professionals" to distinguish themselves from the political appointees who become ambassadors by that route.

Now I ask you, would it be acceptable to members of your profession to have the top practitioners in your field selected by the "spoils system?" Imagine if military commands – the ranks of flag officers – were sold to the highest bidders? Obviously not, although that was once the case, at the time of George Washington.

Just a few words about the history of diplomacy, my former profession.

Diplomacy used to be a kind of game played by aristocrats on behalf of their monarchs.

Many of these early diplomats had fine educations, languages and skills, but they were in no modern sense "professionals." What they were was *loyal servants of the king*.

Sir Henry Wotton, in 1604, famously said that "an ambassador is an honest man sent to lie abroad for the good of his country." That led to some confusion, because "lie abroad" has two meanings in English.

Not for nothing is diplomacy often called "the second oldest profession."

As society changed, diplomacy became the province of wealthy and well-connected individuals who were amateurs for the most part, although often well-qualified. They received little or no salary. Consuls could collect fees, as Nathaniel Hawthorne, the American author, did in Liverpool in the nineteenth century.

Until World War I, Americans aspiring to represent their country had to show *proof of a private income* in order to be considered for assignments as diplomats overseas.

It was not until 1924, through the Rogers Act, that the US Foreign Service was merged with the consular service and put on a more professional basis. Eventually there was a real entrance examination and some serious training was provided.

But still, the idea of the talented "amateur," inherited from the British, dominated. The main way of learning our trade was through "on-the-job training."

On the Continent of Europe, particularly in Germany and Austria, diplomats were expected to have a legal education. The Soviet Union had a diplomatic academy.

Debates have raged for years about the proper training for American diplomats. To this day, technically, no college degree is required to become a Foreign Service Officer, and we still have no official diplomatic academy, although the Foreign Service Institute is now much closer to being one than ever before.

So why am I saying all this? Let me be clear: I have the highest respect for my former colleagues at the State Department and in the Foreign Service. They are professionals in the sense that they know their history, their economics, their political science, languages and many other specialties. They are qualified and talented. In the current atmosphere of criticizing the Federal Government I can only defend them with all my heart.

But there is something else about diplomats. They must be loyal to their employer, the United States Government. The first qualification for a new diplomat is a top secret security clearance.

The key quality that any government wants in its diplomatic employees is loyalty.

So modern diplomats have only one choice of employer: their own country. They have no possibility of working for another.

[This was not always so. In 1862, the Tsar of Russia offered a position in the Russian diplomatic service to Otto von Bismarck, who was just leaving St Petersburg as Ambassador of Prussia. Bismarck courteously declined, but the fact that the Tsar considered it a possibility is, in itself, telling.]

So a big difference between foreign service professionals and other professionals is that they are not free to move to another "firm" as many others in civilian life may do.

In an earlier age, when the diplomats were aristocrats, there existed a certain shared sense of morality, centered on the individual.

In the modern age, the Nation competes with morality for the loyalty even of the individual citizen. So the commandment, "Thou shalt not kill" becomes "Thou shalt not kill, except under certain circumstances" [the enemies of one's country]. Diplomats, unlike soldiers, are not normally involved directly in killing even our enemies, but they may be required to do other things that go against their own personal sense of ethics.

You can probably see where this is leading. So let me cut to the chase.

I faced an *ethical dilemma* when I became the US Ambassador to Armenia, and particularly when I took the trouble to look into the issue of what happened in 1915, and what the Genocide Convention of 1948 really said. I had not known the full facts before.

I responded to the *ethical demand* that I not participate in the systematic denial of the Armenian Genocide, rather than to the *professional demand* that I represent my employer, the Department of State, by cooperating in that policy of denial.

Some of my former colleagues will never forgive me for making that choice.

Others have privately congratulated me, and, as you may know, the American Foreign Service Association selected me for an award, the Christian Herter Award for Constructive Dissent by a senior officer. So far as I know, the United States is the only country which allows an award for "dissent" to be given to its diplomats.

By the way, although that award was rescinded on a technicality, I am still hoping it will be restored to me *posthumously* – just not too soon!

So, to sum up, I believe you are recognizing me not for being a professional, but for violating the modern professional standards of my chosen occupation.

Sometimes we must be guided not by our professional ethics, but by a higher morality.

I thank you for honoring me, and for your attention this evening.

(As prepared for delivery; actual remarks departed from this text)

ANCA Conference Armenian Cause 2.0

Washington, D.C., June 25, 2011

All organizations must adapt to new conditions in order to survive and remain relevant. Think big. Make history while you are here.

You will be looking at ways of being more effective. ANCA is very effective on Capitol Hill. But there is another Washington. Executive Branch. State Department, Defense Department, Embassies, NSC, etc.

These are two completely different worlds:

Congress takes a *short-term* view and aims at reelection. House is worse than the Senate in this. Flattery works in both chambers.

Executive Branch – at least the career people – take a *long view*, essentially have tenure, are meritocratic, have to work with Congress and for either party. They are risk-averse. They work to advance their careers, but also sincerely to advance our country's interests.

Executive Branch is a strong *hierarchy*. Everyone has a boss and even the President's not fully free: he must heed his advisors and associates.

Executive Branch has a team ethic. They stick together, demand loyalty, punish mavericks, or "loose cannons." Value discipline.

Executive Branch – and I speak mainly of the State Department – people are:

* Honest, hard-working, decent, not "evil" or "wicked";
* Smart, not stupid. Respond to facts, not rhetoric or emotions;
* Do not respond to flattery or to simple pressure;
* Most of all, they respond to directives from above them.

This brings me to a conversation I had with Aram [Hamparian] about whether one might "capture" the White House, given that the

Executive Branch is not very susceptible to influence. My contention is that it has already been done. Let me recall how.

It started with a book. Samantha Power's *Genocide: a Problem from Hell.*

A Senator from Illinois read the book and invited Samantha Power to visit him. They talked far longer than expected. He asked her to join his staff.

An Ambassador read the same book, as well as several others, and came out publicly, against stated policy, for recognition of the Armenian Genocide.

This caused the recall of the ambassador (that would be me) and a Senate Hearing to confirm his successor, Richard Hoagland.

In the course of the confirmation process, Senator Obama wrote a letter to Secretary of State Rice affirming the fact of the Genocide and questioning official policy toward it.

Dick Hoagland was not confirmed because another Senator (Menendez) twice exercised his right to put a "hold" on the nomination.

The Senator from Illinois won the 2008 Presidential Election. During the campaign, he promised to recognize the Armenian Genocide. Samantha Power produced a video on YouTube supporting Candidate Obama.

In early April, 2009, President Obama traveled to Turkey, spoke in the Grand National Assembly and gave a news conference. In both venues,he made it clear what his own view of the history was, and declared that his view "had not changed."

On April 24, 2009, President Obama issued a very different sort of statement about the Armenian Genocide. It did not use the word "genocide," but it answered the question of whether there had been any "intent" to destroy the Armenians. This was huge. A big step forward.

Two other things are huge: one was the response received by ANCA from the State Department on the occasion of Masha Yovanovich's confirmation.

Another was the fact that Assistant Secretary of State for Europe Dan Fried referred to the "events of 1915" as a case of "ethnic cleansing" in a Congressional hearing.

Since then, both Assistant Secretary Gordon and Secretary of State Clinton have made "unofficial" visits to the Genocide Memorial in Yerevan. This is nothing less than a sea change. And there is more to come.

Honesty in Diplomacy[*]

TEDx Talk, Yerevan, 24 September 2011

It's a great pleasure to be back in Yerevan, and what better spot to talk about honesty in diplomacy? Some of you may think this title is a joke. How many of you think there is honesty in diplomacy? Can I have a show of hands? Does anybody think there is? Not so many. By the way, I wanted to tell you that I am in native dress [I am wearing a suit]. This is native diplomatic dress… just so you know.

The idea that diplomacy is a dirty business, that it is dishonest, goes far back. There was an eminent Elizabethan, Sir Henry Wotton, who famously wrote that "an ambassador is an honest man sent to lie abroad for his country." Now what people don't realize is that there is a little bit of word-play there, because "lie abroad" also refers to "sleep around," or as people may say today, "hook up," and it's true in the courtly diplomacy of the Elizabethan century that there was a lot of court intrigue, and seducing the king's mistress might have been a good way to get information.

And information is what diplomats generally deal in. They are in the information business. Now diplomacy is also sometimes called the second oldest profession. But we diplomats have always known, we professional diplomats, not the ones who made a lot of money selling used cars and donated money to one party or the other and got the job that way, but the professional diplomats who study to become diplomats, who are taught by their elders, who are apprenticed and so on… the real professionals, that we are honest with each other. It's a demand of the profession.

The 17th-century French diplomatist, Callières, wrote a treatise on diplomacy in which he said that "no true diplomat ever tells a falsehood." I would add to that, that a diplomat not only has to be truthful but accurate and up-to-date. Any diplomat who fails to read

---

[*] This is the text of a presentation John Evans delivered at a TEXx talk in Yerevan. For the actual presentation please visit *http://youtu.be/wD86h5L6Hks*

the newspapers in the morning, who fails to be up-to-date with the world's latest situations, and so on, is not going to be consulted either by other diplomats or by his own government. When you are representing your country, you do not dare to destroy your own personal credibility or that of the government you represent. Credibility is the currency of diplomacy.

Now there is a difference between honesty among professionals and the question of confidentiality. Diplomats, as a rule, practice their trade of communicating between governments, reporting back to their governments, informing other governments... as a rule they practice this profession with the protection of confidentiality. That's what the secret codes and the methods of communication are all about. Recently, with Wikileaks, we have had an unprecedented collapse of this veil of confidentiality. And what does it show us? Mostly what it has shown us is that the things – and I can only speak about the Americans because Wikileaks affected the confidentiality of American diplomatic reporting – by and large did not surprise anybody because they described situations that journalists and scholars and others were also describing. Now, occasionally there is a little bit of extra flavor in some of these reports. There might even be some humor.

One of the reports that got a lot of attention was describing a wedding in Dagestan that was really quite unusual, for all sorts of reasons. But the diplomats were reporting accurately and honestly what they saw or heard or what they were told. Where the difficulty has come in for certain parties – and I will give an example, a real life example – that is President Saleh of Yemen, who, in Wikileaks, has now been revealed to have admitted to the U.S. Embassy that he lied to his own Parliament about who was running the drones around Yemen. Now Yemen today is in the throes of a kind of a revolution. In North Africa, one of the leaked cables confirmed for the Tunisians what they all knew about the ruling family there... that there was rampant corruption, nepotism and so on, and the description of it added fuel to the fire there. The same kind of thing happened in Libya. But it is not because the diplomats were dishonest; it's because they told the truth, and the truth was revealed through the lapse of confidentiality occasioned by Wikileaks. Now in a couple of cases that I know about, two American ambassadors have had to leave their posts, Carlos Pasqual from Mexico City and Heather Hodges from Columbia. Not because what they reported was untrue but precisely because it was all too true and the governments there didn't like it at all and in fact went to the White House in the case of Carlos and complained. So two of our ambassadors had to be recalled and replaced by other people.

One American scholar, John Mearscheimer, who is professor of International Relations at the University of Chicago – you may know him, or know of him – before Wikileaks really happened, started to write a book about lying in international relations. He thought there would be lots of examples of this and what he discovered was that there were very few, in fact. States generally, and their representatives, meaning their diplomats, don't lie to each other. Why? The professional considerations that I have already mentioned but also because over a period of time they are going to be found out. It's not easy to keep up a lie, and the cost of a country's lying can be great. Now there are examples of it. It has happened in certain situations. Diplomats of one state, or statesmen of one state, have misled others usually for reasons that they thought overcame the downside or the opprobrium attached to the lying. But what Mearscheimer has found – and his book ended up being called "Why Leaders Lie" – his discovery was this: that it is not the practitioners of diplomacy who are misleading anyone. Dictators, we know, lie, but so do democratic leaders! He gives five examples. I will mention them quickly. They are all American.

The first one: Franklin Roosevelt, in 1941, lied to the American public about the circumstances under which an American naval vessel was sunk in the Atlantic. He did it to build consensus for going to war against Germany. In the end, of course, the Japanese took care of that at Pearl Harbor and we got into World War II. The second example he gave was of Dwight Eisenhower, who lied about the U-2 spy plane, piloted by Gary Powers, who was shot down over the

Soviet Union. The third example was Lyndon Johnson in describing to the American public the events in the Gulf of Tonkin in the build-up to Vietnam. Another example, well, there is an example of what we are *not* discussing today and that is Bill Clinton talking about Monica Lewinsky. Let's leave that to the side. In terms of international relations that is a fairly inconsequential kind of lie of the sort that, you know, gentlemen in the audience, if your wife asks you "does this dress make me look fat?" you're going to lie. That's different. And then a final example, which actually has been mentioned here today, is that of the Bush-Cheney Administration which, Mearscheimer says, told basically four lies as we were going into the Iraq war. Now I am not going to get into that either. You can find the book if you are interested. It's called "Why Leaders Lie" and was published by Oxford University Press this year [2011].

So where does this take us? What it tells us is that leaders do mislead their publics. Now, usually, or when it happens, they are doing it because they think they know better about something in the international environment. They think their publics will not follow them into a certain policy unless they very much exaggerate the threat. This is a kind of policy lie. It's a lie designed to make a certain policy choice more desirable or more acceptable to the public. But then, there is another kind of lie, a bigger kind of a lie. And that is – as Balzac said, "every great family fortune is based on a great crime" – well, many nation-states are also based on either a crime, or call it a victory. In some cases it's a defeat. The Armenians being defeated by the Persians in 451 might be considered one of those founding moments. When the Serbs were defeated at Kosovo Pole in 1387... defeated... that is considered by Serbs to be the founding of their nation. It is one reason they are so attached politically, emotionally and culturally to Kosovo. These myths are what states lie about in the deepest and most harmful way.

We in the United States, of course, have our founding myth. We have a mixture of myths, actually. How the good Englishmen – they usually don't talk about the other nationalities – the good Englishmen came to Virginia and met the Indians, of course some of the Indians came and attacked us, but we basically took their land. So there is the myth, or story, that we tell about winning the West. We don't talk about a 400-year rolling genocide. And admittedly, not all of it was genocidal under the definition that we have. There were attacks in both directions. But we do know, and we have written instructions of one British officer [Lord Jeffrey Amherst] to send infected, smallpox-infected blankets to a village to kill the inhabitants of that village. That was a genocidal act. We don't talk about that very much. And there are other countries… as no one in this room in Yerevan needs to be reminded… that were founded on a great crime, or a great victory, whichever way you put it.

I, six years ago, decided to call it a crime. You know what I am talking about. But maybe the lesson today is to understand what a huge lie this is and how difficult it is for the Turks to get beyond that enormous lie which, with each year that passes, becomes more difficult because the wrong story has been taught to yet another crop of students, of school children. So this is a very difficult issue, as we all know, but I do not believe that problems of this sort can be solved by silence. We have to look at the truth. It is in our nature as human beings. Now I remember in one meeting in 2005 in Washington, a Turkish ambassador who was visiting said "you know, each nation creates the history that it needs as a nation and that's why the Armenians say there was a genocide. There was no genocide! If we had wanted to kill them all, we would have used bullets!" He was talking about Armenian myth-making. This is very, very difficult stuff.

What I was trying to do six years ago, and I am so grateful to Civilitas to have invited me back five years after I left, particularly at this time and to such a wonderful event. But what I was trying to do then concerned a taboo. We didn't have an instruction from the Secretary of State saying "you may not talk about this subject." We just had deeply misleading talking points that we were supposed to deploy and they started out by saying "no U.S. official has ever denied the facts of what happened in 1915." Never mind that none of us in the early days really knew what the facts were! The scholarship on the Armenian genocide has increased so amazingly in the last 20 years. But 25 years ago, hardly anybody knew about it. Nor did many of our professional diplomats know about the Genocide Convention that was signed by the United States in 1948 but only ratified in 1988. And why did it take so long? Because there were certain senators, Southern senators, who feared that the Genocide Convention could be used against the United States in the matter of lynching.

So where does this bring us? I think we have to challenge ourselves to understand the role of myths in our lives, in our political lives, to understand that these are difficult problems that can't be solved by silence. They can only be solved when they are discussed in an open way. And one final thought. The subject of today's conference is supposedly "becoming young." I think you know when we're young, we're idealistic. The idealism gets beaten out of us over the years, particularly if we are in a large institution, but at some point you may come to the realization that it is not enough just to do your job, even to do your job well, but to stand for something, something that might make a little bit of a change, and you go back to that youthful idealism, a different concept of morality than the professional strictures that are inculcated in us. I hope every one of you will consider, yourselves, what you can do. Thank you for your attention, and God bless you all.

Post-Script

John Evans, Washington, D.C., February, 2016

War and genocide are persistent troublesome facts of human existence.

A team of archeologists from Cambridge has discovered a prehistoric site of carnage of hunter-gatherers in Nataruk, in what is now Kenya, that dates intercommunal violence to at least 10,000 years ago. Probably such violence is even older in the human story, and did not begin, as has been hypothesized, only when Man began to till the land. (cam.ac.uk)

We know from more recent history what violence an Imperial Power or an expanding State or a tottering autocracy can perpetrate on its enemies, foreign or domestic, for the sake of power, land or religion. But when a group of states pursue their various goals through well-armed and well-financed proxies, as has recently been happening in Syria and Iraq, the results are devastating, and we see them via the internet. There is no doubt in my mind that genocidal episodes have been taking place, in Syria in particular, in the past year or two. Tragically, the descendants of those who escaped the Armenian Genocide for the relative safety of Aleppo and Deir-ez-Zor are again becoming victims, as have other Christians – the Assyrians, the Chaldeans, the Copts, the Syrian Orthodox—and, to be fair, the Yazidis, Shiites and Sunnis alike. The similarities to the 1915 Christian Genocide are eerie: churches and monasteries demolished, women and children enslaved, the jizya (tax on non-Muslims) imposed, priests beheaded. And Turkish troops, in the process of devastating a village (Silopi) in eastern Turkey, sing "We will kill all Kurds as we have slaughtered all the Armenians. Amen!"[*]

The question, it seems, is not "when will this end?" but "will it ever end?"

---

[*] YouTube 1/24/2016

On the evidence, it looks probable that not only wars (and undeclared military actions, hyper-wars, and drone attacks) but the genocides that so often accompany them, will continue well into the future of our violent species.

That is on the evidence.

Damn the evidence!

We, those of us with any sense of decency left, must ignore the evidence and do, each of us, whatever we can to improve the odds for peace, justice and sanity in this world, or we ourselves will be damned.

If we cannot say – and mean – "never again," what we are left with is "ever again, and again."

END

John M. Evans, *Truth Held Hostage: America and the Armenian Genocide - What Then? What Now?* with a foreword by Dickran Kouymjian, London: Gomidas Institute, 2016, 200 pp., photos, maps, index. ISBN 9781909382268

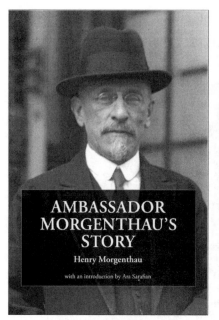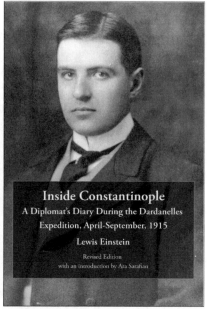

TWO AMERICAN OFFICIALS WHO SPOKE OUT AGAINST THE ARMENIAN GENOCIDE DURING WWI

Henry Morgenthau, *Ambassador Morgenthau's Story*, London: Gomidas Institute, 2016, 310 pp., photos, map. ISBN 978-1-909382-21-3

Lewis Einstein, *Inside Constantinople: A Diplomatist's Diary During the Dardanelles Expedition, April - September 1915,* London: Gomidas Institute, 2015, 204 pp., map, illustr., index., ISBN 978-1-909382-11-4

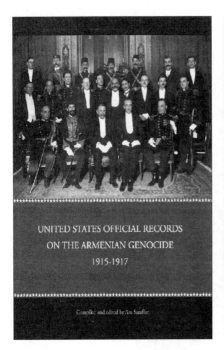

AMERICAN ARCHIVAL SOURCES ON THE
ARMENIAN GENOCIDE

Henry Morgenthau, *United States Diplomacy on the Bosphorus: The Diaries of Ambassador Morgenthau, 1913-1916*, London: Gomidas Institute, 2004, xviii + 500 pp, photos and maps, ISBN 1-903656-40-0

Ara Sarafian (comp. ed and intro), *United States Official Records on the Armenian Genocide 1915-1917*, London: Gomidas Institute, 2004, xxxvi + 706 pp., illust., maps, ISBN 1-903656-39-7

GOMIDAS INSTITUTE
42 BLYTHE RD.
LONDON W14 0HA
ENGLAND

www.gomidas.org